THE HISTORY OF SPACE EXPLORATION

SPACE SHUTTLES

ROBIN KERROD

WORLD ALMANAC® LIBRARY

Please visit our web site at:
www.worldalmanaclibrary.com
For a free color catalog describing
World Almanac® Library's list of high-quality
books and multimedia programs, call
1-800-848-2928 (USA) or 1-800-387-3178
(Canada). World Almanac® Library's fax:
(414) 332-3567.

Library of Congress Cataloging-in-Publication Data

Kerrod, Robin.
    Space shuttles / by Robin Kerrod.
       p. cm. — (The history of space exploration)
    Includes bibliographical references and index.
    ISBN 0-8368-5709-7 (lib. bdg.)
    ISBN 0-8368-5716-X (softcover)
    1. Space shuttles—Juvenile literature. I. Title.
II. Series.
    TL795.515.K47   2004
    629.44'1—dc22   2004049217

First published in 2005 by
World Almanac® Library
330 West Olive Street, Suite 100
Milwaukee, WI 53212 USA

Developed by White-Thomson Publishing Ltd.
Editor: Veronica Ross
Designer: Gary Frost, Leishman Design
Picture researcher: Elaine Fuoco-Lang

World Almanac® Library editor: Carol Ryback
World Almanac® Library designer: Kami Koenig
World Almanac® Library art direction: Tammy West

Photo credits: top (t), bottom (b), left (l), right (r)
All images used with the permission of NASA except:
CORBIS 36, 40. Space Charts Photo Library; 8, 9, 13,
15, 16, 17, 18, 21(b), 25(b), 27(t), 34, 37, 43(t).

Printed in Canada

1 2 3 4 5 6 7 8 9 09 08 07 06 05 04

Cover image: Space shuttle Columbia *lifting off the
launch pad in April 1981.*

Title page: Space Shuttle Endeavour *touches down
on the runway after its maiden flight.*

*Contents page: Bruce McCandless testing the manned
maneuvering unit (MMR) in February 1984.*

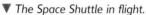

▼ *The Space Shuttle in flight.*

CONTENTS

COMMUTING INTO SPACE

Until 1981, every U.S. astronaut or Soviet cosmonaut had traveled into space in launch vehicles that were expendable: They could be used only once. The only parts that came back to Earth were the tiny capsules containing the crews. This method of launching represented a huge waste of resources. It would surely be much better—and cheaper—to travel to and from space in vehicles that could be reused time after time.

The National Aeronautics and Space Administration's (NASA's) reusable Space Shuttle made its debut on April 12, 1981, when *Columbia* blasted off for the first time. Seven months later, it headed back into space—as no craft had ever done before. By the end of 2002, Space Shuttles had made more than 110 flights into space and back.

The Shuttle has proved an exciting development in spaceflight, able to carry a large crew and a large payload (cargo) into orbit. There have been many triumphs, such as the in-orbit recovery and repair of satellites by space-walking astronauts. But the Space Shuttle program has also experienced its share of tragedy: *Challenger* exploded during liftoff in January 1986; *Columbia* broke up when coming in for a landing in February 2003.

Soviet space scientists also developed a nearly identical Space Shuttle called *Buran*, but after just one unmanned flight in 1988, they abandoned this project.

Shuttles will probably continue to fly until at least the end of this decade, when other spacecraft will join them in the skies. These will include much simpler and much cheaper space vehicles, such as the Orbital Space Plane, which is launched by expendable rockets.

▶ *Riding on a pillar of flame and smoke, Space Shuttle* Atlantis *thunders into the Florida sky in September 1997. In only about twenty minutes,* Atlantis *will be traveling silently in orbit around Earth.*

CHAPTER ONE

TESTING TIMES

President Richard M. Nixon approved the Space Shuttle program in 1972, when the present Shuttle system design was almost finalized. Even then, the idea of reusable launch vehicles was nothing new.

Early ideas about rocket-boosted winged vehicles that could be reused originated in Germany in the late 1930s and early 1940s. Wernher von Braun's rocket team that developed the infamous V-2 rocket bomb used in World War II (1939–1945) also considered plans for a two-stage launch vehicle. Its upper-rocket stage would be fitted with wings to extend its range by gliding.

At the time, German engineer Eugen Sänger and his wife, mathematician Irene Bredt, presented their design for an "antipodal bomber"—so-called because they believed it could reach the antipodes, or the other side of the world. It would be launched by a rocket-

▲ An HL-10 lifting-body craft in flight in January 1969, after being dropped from a B-52 aircraft.

powered sledge, which would provide its initial speed. Then it would fire its own rocket engines, increasing its speed and boosting it to a height of about 100 miles (160 kilometers). It would glide back into the atmosphere at a shallow angle, skipping in and out like a flat stone thrown across the surface of a pond, before finally landing 10,000 miles (16,000 km) away.

THE DYNA SOAR

In 1958, when the United States entered the Space Age, the U.S. Air Force took up Sänger's ideas in a project known as Dyna Soar (for "dynamic ascent and soaring flight"). Later called the X-20, Dyna Soar was a glider designed to be boosted into orbit on a Titan III rocket. It was fitted with retrorockets, which fired near the end of the mission to slow the glider down before it reentered the atmosphere and glided down onto a runway. The United States cancelled the project in 1963 because of NASA's push into space with expendable Mercury, Gemini, and Apollo spacecraft.

LIFTING BODIES

By then, however, research into what became known as lifting bodies was underway at the NASA Flight Research Center (now the Dryden Flight Research Center) at Edwards Air Force Base in California. Lifting bodies were designed so that they could fly back to Earth from space, be maneuvered

▲ Experimental lifting-body craft on the runway at the NASA (now Dryden) Flight Research Center in California. From left to right, they are the X-24A, M2-F3, and the HL-10.

DRYDEN FLIGHT RESEARCH CENTER

Some of the nation's greatest advances in aviation occurred at the Hugh L. Dryden Flight Research Center at Edwards, California, 80 miles (130 km) north of Los Angeles. Established in 1946, it is adjacent to Rogers Dry Lake, which provides a flat natural surface for aircraft landings about 44 square miles (114 square km) in area. Dryden served as the flying base for a host of experimental aircraft. They include the Bell X-1, in which Chuck Yeager in 1947 first flew at Mach 1—the speed of sound—to "break the sound barrier." Lifting bodies, X-15 rocket planes, and the prototype Space Shuttle *Enterprise* are among the many craft flight tested at Dryden.

in the atmosphere, and land like an airplane on a runway. They were blunt-nosed, wingless vehicles, with a shape that produced lift when they traveled through the atmosphere. "Lift" is an upward force that acts against the downward force of gravity to support bodies (including airplanes) flying through the air. Tests began on a prototype lifting body, the M2-F1, in 1963.

Successful ground-tow and aircraft-tow tests of the M2-F1 led to the development of further lifting-body craft, the M2-F2, the HL-10, the X-24A, and X-24B. They were involved in manned flight tests in which they were dropped from a converted B-52 bomber.

HIGHER AND FASTER

The later versions of the lifting-body designs were equipped with rocket engines, designed to assist maneuverability when coming in to land. But other craft were using their rocket engines to explore flight at high altitude and at very high speeds. They were the X-15s, which were air launched from a B-52.

▼ A B-52 aircraft carries an X-15 under its wing in January 1965. It will release the rocket plane at an altitude of about 45,000 feet (13,700 meters).

By the time its test flights finished in October 1968, X-15s had reached altitudes of more than 350,000 feet (107,000 m) and achieved hypersonic speeds of nearly seven times the speed of sound, or Mach 7.

EARLY SHUTTLE CONCEPTS

The history of the Space Shuttle as we know it today began early in April 1969, three months before the first Apollo astronauts set foot on the Moon.

President Richard M. Nixon asked NASA's Space Task Group to plan the course of the American space program after Apollo. It decided that the first priority was to develop a reusable space transportation system and recommended this to the President. He approved, and studies began on possible designs.

At first, NASA considered a fully reusable shuttle. It would consist of a two-stage vehicle with both

▲ A 1972 NASA artist's impression of the Space Shuttle taking off. By that time, the modern Shuttle design was more or less finalized.

▲ An artist's rendition of a fully reusable shuttle (1970), presented by North American Rockwell, the company that eventually won the contract to build the Space Shuttle Fleet. As the orbiter powers its way into space, the winged booster portion returns to Earth.

stages manned. Each stage would use rocket engines for power and have delta-shaped wings for flying. Delta wings, triangular wings shaped like the Greek capital letter delta "Δ," provide plenty of lift at high speeds. The two-stage shuttle would take off vertically from the launchpad. The craft's booster stage would lift it high into the atmosphere. After separation from the orbiter, the booster stage could return to base for a runway landing.

The upper, orbiter stage (the part of the shuttle that carried the crew) would meanwhile fire its own rocket engines, thrusting it into orbit. When the mission was complete, the orbiter would reenter the atmosphere and also make a runway landing.

HIGH COSTS

The high cost of this fully reusable system eventually doomed it, and NASA switched to the idea of using unmanned, recoverable, and recyclable booster rockets. The orbiter design changed as well. Engineers concentrated on developing a much smaller vehicle that used a fuel supply from a disposable, external tank.

President Nixon gave approval for a mostly reusable Space Shuttle on January 5, 1972. Two months later, designers decided that the boosters would use solid instead of liquid propellants (the substances burned in a rocket to propel it). Solid boosters proved much simpler in design and also more economical than liquid ones. They were also sturdier and easier to refurbish for repeated use.

> ". . . the United States should proceed at once with the development of an entirely new type of space transportation system designed to help transform the space frontier of the 1970s into familiar territory, easily accessible for human endeavor in the 1980s and '90s. . . . It will revolutionize transportation in near space by routinizing it. It will take the astronomical costs out of astronautics. . . . This is why commitment to the Space Shuttle program is the right step for America to take."
>
> **U.S. president Nixon, January 5, 1972.**

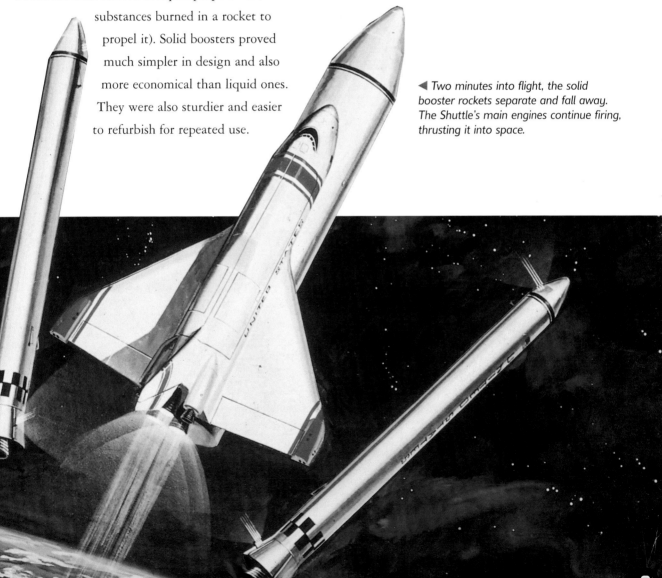

◀ *Two minutes into flight, the solid booster rockets separate and fall away. The Shuttle's main engines continue firing, thrusting it into space.*

OFF THE DRAWING BOARD

By March 1972, all the elements of the Space Shuttle, or Space Transportation System, fell into place:

1. A winged orbiter to carry the crew and payload (cargo);
2. An external tank to hold the main orbiter's propellants and to jettison when empty;
3 Twin solid rocket boosters (SRBs)—strapped to the external tank at liftoff—that would parachute back to Earth for recovery.

Work began on the detailed Shuttle design. As with any major government project, the company or companies that hoped to build these spacecraft submitted bids (cost estimates) for the job. North American Rockwell Corporation (now Rockwell International) became the main contractor for the orbiter; Thiokol Chemical Corporation and McDonnell Douglas, for the solid rocket boosters; and Martin Marietta, for the external tank.

ORBITER DESIGN

Wind-tunnel tests and data obtained from the flights of the lifting bodies and the X-15 rocket planes helped determine the final design of the orbiter.

NASA hoped that the first Shuttle flight could occur as early as 1977 but the first Shuttle orbiter was finally rolled out that year instead. The craft, a prototype named *Enterprise*, was destined only for atmospheric flights.

▶ *Wind-tunnel testing of a small-scale Shuttle model. Wind tunnel test results provide a good idea of how an actual craft will behave when lifting off and returning through the atmosphere.*

▼ *Space Shuttle* Enterprise *in 1977, with cast of the TV series,* Star Trek. *Their characters "boldly [went] where no [one] had gone before," in the starship USS* Enterprise.

ENTERPRISE

U.S. president Gerald Ford named the prototype orbiter *Enterprise* after the famous starship of the *Star Trek* television (and later film) series. Although *Enterprise* was the first orbiter to fly in the atmosphere, it never flew in space—much less at "warp speeds" between galaxies.

APPROACH AND LANDING TESTS

Enterprise made its first flight on top of a converted Boeing 747 carrier aircraft in February 1977. In August, several free flights from the 747 set the orbiters on flight paths that ended with runway landings at the Edwards Air Force Base.

By the time the approach and landing tests were completed in October, *Enterprise*'s aerodynamic design had proved flawless. NASA hoped that the first Shuttle space flight would occur in 1979.

▲ Enterprise *glides smoothly through the atmosphere on one of its thirteen approach and landing test missions in 1977. It never flew in space.*

A number of design difficulties with the entirely new main engines and with the manufacture of the ceramic tiles that formed the Shuttle's heat shield kept the project grounded.

ROLL-OUT

After its successful atmospheric flights, *Enterprise* flew to the Marshall Space Flight Center in Huntsville, Alabama, for eight months of vibration tests. The tests subjected the orbiter's structure to the types of vibrations a working orbiter would experience during a real space flight. The tests would reveal any problems with the design and construction of the vehicle. In April 1979, *Enterprise* arrived at the Kennedy Space Center in Florida, where launch Complex 39 was being readied for the Space Shuttle era.

A "Shuttle stack," with *Enterprise* joined to an external tank and solid rocket boosters, rolled out of the enormous Vehicle Assembly Building (VAB) on May 1. Nearly two years later, *Columbia*, the first operational orbiter, thundered from the launchpad.

CHAPTER TWO

FIRST FLIGHTS

The construction and successful approach and landing tests of *Enterprise* cleared the way to build the operational Shuttles. The first Space Shuttle made its triumphant debut on the twentieth anniversary of the first manned flight into space by Soviet cosmonaut Yuri Gagarin.

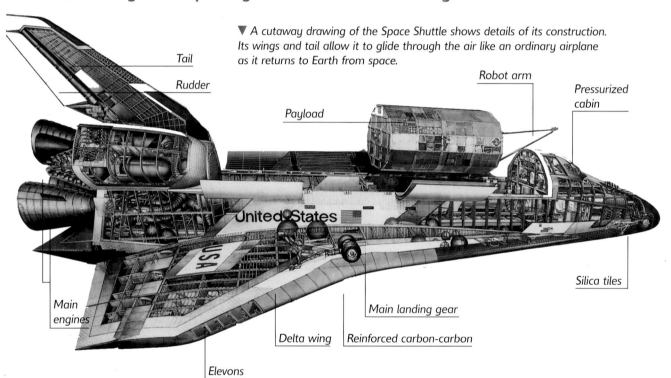

▼ A cutaway drawing of the Space Shuttle shows details of its construction. Its wings and tail allow it to glide through the air like an ordinary airplane as it returns to Earth from space.

Tail

Rudder

Payload

Robot arm

Pressurized cabin

United States

USA

Silica tiles

Main engines

Main landing gear

Delta wing

Reinforced carbon-carbon

Elevons

The orbiter is the part of the Space Shuttle Transportation System that carries the crew. It looks like a small commercial airplane, but with stubby, delta wings near its tail. The Shuttle's orbiter measures 122 feet (37 m) long, making it smaller than a Boeing 737 and only about half the size of a jumbo jet.

Orbiter construction is surprisingly conventional considering that it is designed to fly at incredibly high speeds through outer space and in Earth's atmosphere. Its airframe, or main body, consists mostly of aluminum alloys (mixtures of one or more metals). Certain areas, such as the orbiter's wing edges, belly, tail, and nose, that are expected to experience high stresses or that must withstand extremely high temperatures, are built from high-strength materials such as titanium or reinforced carbon-carbon.

HEAT SHIELDING

During atmospheric reentry, air friction causes temperatures on the exterior of the orbiter to soar. For protection, a variety of insulating materials cover the airframe. The nose and leading edges of the wings experience the highest temperatures—more than 2,700 degrees Fahrenheit (1,500 degrees Celsius).

THE FLYING BRICKYARD

Workers nicknamed *Columbia* "the flying brickyard" because of the 30,000 ceramic tiles that covered its exterior. Composed of special purified sand, or silica, the numbered tiles fit into specific places on every craft like giant jigsaw pieces. Technicians carefully examine each tile for dents, nicks, or missing pieces after every Shuttle mission. Any damaged tiles are replaced before that Shuttle orbiter flies again.

▼ *The Shuttle's silica-tile material provides extraordinary insulation. Though still white-hot inside, this sample is still cool to the touch because the heat has not traveled through to the outside.*

▲ *A Space Shuttle under construction at Rockwell's facility in Downey, California, in 1979. Thick black insulating tiles cover the areas that will experience the greatest heat stresses when the Shuttle orbiter reenters the atmosphere after a spaceflight.*

A carbon-based material called reinforced carbon-carbon (RCC) protects these vulnerable areas and was selected because it resists high temperatures. A coating of a silicon carbide, which does not oxidize (combine with oxygen), prevents the RCC from deteriorating in the extreme heat. Thick black tiles made from silica cover the underside of the orbiter. Silica—the same mineral found in sand—also withstands high temperatures. Thinner white silica tiles or insulating felt cover most of the upper side.

CONTROLLING FLIGHT

The orbiter's design helps control its flight path through the atmosphere. Wings provide lift. The tail fin and rudder provide stable flight. Flaps, or elevons, at the rear of the wings, provide directional control.

SHUTTLE ENGINES

The orbiter has three powerful main engines that burn liquid hydrogen and liquid oxygen as propellants. The two substances react to produce

water, or (more correctly) water vapor. The main
engines fire together at liftoff, along with the solid
rocket boosters, producing more than 1 million
pounds (500,000 kilograms) of thrust. To do this
they must consume propellants at the rate of about
63,000 gallons (290,000 liters) a minute. (If they
sucked water from a family swimming pool at this
rate, they would empty it in less than half a minute.)

The propellants are fed to the main engines from
the huge external fuel tank. With a length of 154
feet (47 m), it is the longest item of Shuttle hardware
and the only one discarded in flight. It holds more
than 500,000 gallons (2 million l) of liquid hydrogen
and liquid oxygen.

THE SRBs

The two solid rocket boosters, or SRBs, provide
most of the liftoff thrust. They burn for about two
minutes before separating and parachuting back
to Earth for recovery. The 149-foot (45.4-m) -long
SRBs are made of steel segments joined together.
A parachute is stored in each nose cone.

The solid propellant used in the SRBs is a mixture
of aluminum powder, acting as fuel, with an
ammonium compound acting as an oxidizer to burn
the fuel. These substances are blended into a type
of synthetic rubber binder. When the SRBs burn,
they produce a lot of flames and smoke, unlike the
transparent blue flame of the Shuttle's main engines.

▼ A Shuttle takes to the air with all engines blazing.
The two solid rocket boosters provide the main thrust.
They will soon drop away, leaving the Shuttle's three
main engines to lift the craft into space.

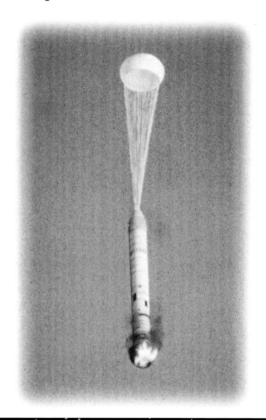

▼ A solid rocket booster descends by parachute toward the ocean. It will be picked up by a recovery ship and returned to the Kennedy Space Center for refurbishing and reuse.

SHUTTLE POWER

Two main systems provide the power to operate all the hundreds of systems that make the orbiter work. One is the hydraulic power system. This provides liquid under pressure ("hydraulic pressure") to operate such devices as the wing flaps, rudder, landing gear, and wheel brakes. The hydraulic power is provided by turbine-driven pumps, known as the APUs (auxiliary power units). Three fuel-cell power units provide electrical power to run the computers, lights, equipment, and life-support systems. Fuel cells produce electricity from a chemical reaction between hydrogen and oxygen, which combine to form water. The water is pure and suitable for the crew to use for cooking and washing.

OMS AND RCS

Also in the tail of the orbiter are two smaller engines of the orbital maneuvering system (OMS). The OMS engines are fired briefly to put the Shuttle into orbit and fired again as retrorockets to slow down the craft so that it drops down from orbit at the mission's end. The other engines on the orbiter are the sets of little thrusters of the reaction control system (RCS). There are two sets of RCS thrusters alongside the other engines in the tail as well as sets in the nose. They are fired when necessary to control the orbiter's attitude, or orientation, in space.

▲ Just before a Space Shuttle enters orbit, it jettisons the external tank, which plunges into the ocean.

CREW AND PAYLOAD

The Shuttle crew lives and works in a pressurized cabin in the front fuselage of the orbiter. The mid-deck area provides the crew's accommodations. The Shuttle commander and pilot fly the orbiter from the flight deck, or cockpit, at the front of the upper deck of the crew cabin.

The cockpit looks like that of a modern jet airliner, but with many more instruments and controls. It also has three video display screens that are linked to the onboard computer system, so that the astronauts can access information about any aspect of the flight or the orbiter's systems.

The Shuttle's payload, or cargo, is carried in the unpressurized payload bay behind the crew cabin. The payload bay measures 60 feet long by 15 feet across (18 m by 4.6 m). Payload operations are controlled from the payload station at the rear of the upper deck, where windows allow a view of the payload bay. Astronauts often use the Shuttle's "crane" to help them handle payloads. Called the Remote Manipulator System (RMS), it is a 50-foot (15-m) long robot arm with flexible joints.

THE SPACE CADILLAC

The Shuttle is certainly the most advanced flying machine ever. But it has failed in its promise to

▲ Mounted on a mobile launch platform, Columbia rolls toward its launchpad more than 3 miles (5 km) away on December 29, 1980.

provide an economical access to space. Even before the first Shuttle flight, critics described it as a needlessly large and complex vehicle.

The perceived need of carrying both people and payloads dictated its design. A crew-carrying vehicle is always complicated because it must protect its occupants during launch, spaceflight, and reentry. It needs a pressurized cabin, an environmental control system, heat shielding, and so on. It also needs emergency backup systems—the Shuttle has five computers, for example.

Originally, designers thought the Shuttle would provide a cheaper method for launching satellites than using ordinary expendable launch vehicles (ELVs), like the Delta and Titan. But some critics compared using the sophisticated Shuttle for launching satellites to using a Cadillac as a delivery vehicle. The cost of using the Shuttle as a satellite-launching vehicle caused many companies to switch to alternative launch vehicles, such as the ESA's Ariane rockets.

▲ Space Shuttle Columbia is lowered into position on the Shuttle stack inside the Vehicle Assembly Building at the Kennedy Space Center in December 1980.

▲ *On launchpad Complex 39A, technicians work at night to prepare* Columbia *for its maiden voyage into space.*

FIRST FLIGHT

The first operational Space Shuttle was named *Columbia* after a sailing ship that became famous for being the first U.S. ship to circumnavigate the globe.

Columbia arrived at the Kennedy Space Center on board a 747 carrier jet early in March 1979. But it did not roll out to the launchpad until December 1980 and was not ready for launch until the morning of April 10, 1981.

Veteran astronaut John Young and rookie Robert Crippen were selected as the crew for *Columbia*'s first mission (*STS-1*). The men would in a very real sense be test pilots, for they would be testing a radically new spacecraft and launch system. Each part—orbiter, SRBs, external tank—had undergone tests

COMPLEX 39

Space Shuttles launch from Complex 39 at the Kennedy Space Center. Complex 39 was built to accommodate the Saturn V/Apollo launches to the Moon in the 1960s and early 1970s. The huge Vehicle Assembly Building, built as an assembly area for the Saturn V/Apollo stack and now modified to assemble the Space Shuttle stack, dominates the site. As in Apollo days, a stack is mounted on a mobile launch platform, a huge crawler transporter, nicknamed the "mighty tortoise," for the move to launchpads 39A or 39B.

separately on the ground, but they had never been tested together and flown in space. On the morning of April 10, 1981, hundreds of thousands of spectators gathered in and around the Kennedy Space Center and in outlying areas and waited to

see if this revolutionary new space launch system would fly.

The countdown went smoothly until T-9, only nine minutes left before takeoff. At that time there was a built-in "hold," when the countdown was halted temporarily as final checks were made. On that day, the countdown never resumed because technicians discovered faults in *Columbia*'s computer system. The launch was cancelled.

A countdown for a launch two days later progressed to zero, and a little after 7:00 A.M. (local time), *Columbia* lifted off the launchpad on a pillar of flame, steam, and smoke. The Space Shuttle, developed at a cost of about $10 billion, was airborne at last.

Two minutes after liftoff, the SRBs separated and fell away. *Columbia*'s main engines continued firing for another six minutes, and then the external tank separated and fell away. A short burst of the OMS

▲ *On April 11, 1981, thousands of people gather along the roads to the Kennedy Space Center. Liftoff of the first Space Shuttle is scheduled for the next morning. The spectators are about 5 miles (8 km) from the launchpad.*

engines put *Columbia* into an orbit about 170 miles (275 km) high.

BACK HOME

Cameras showed that a number of insulating tiles fell off the Shuttle's tail fin during launch. Vibrations, air-flow forces, or friction may have knocked them loose. Otherwise, the craft was in excellent shape. NASA cleared the crew for the scheduled thirty-six orbit mission.

On the thirty-sixth orbit, the crew maneuvered *Columbia* to flip out of its upside-down and backward-facing position. They then fired the OMS engines to slow it down. Soon the *Columbia* was slamming into the air of the upper atmosphere at twenty-five times the speed of sound. No other winged craft had ever attempted this feat. Air friction heated up the surface of *Columbia* to temperatures as high as 2,700° F (1,500° C).

▼ *Just after 7 A.M., on April 12, 1981,* Columbia *lifts off the launchpad and thunders into the heavens. The first* Space Shuttle *mission (STS-1) is underway.*

Communications with *Columbia* suddenly ceased—it entered a "communications blackout" in which radio waves could not enter or leave the craft. This always occurs when air around a spacecraft becomes so hot that it ionizes: All the air molecules surrounding the vehicle take on an electrical charge. Radio waves cannot pass through ionized air.

For twenty-one minutes there was nothing but noisy interference on Mission Control's speakers. Then came Young's voice: "Hello Houston, *Columbia* here." The brand-new spacecraft survived perhaps the worst part of the mission. About fifty-four hours after liftoff, *Columbia* touched down at Edwards Air Force Base. Its near-flawless mission signaled the dawn of a new era in spaceflight.

▲ *During the first Shuttle flight, commander John Young is pictured in* Columbia's *cockpit. A veteran of the Gemini and Apollo eras, he is making a record fifth flight into space.*

This vehicle is behaving like a champ. I've got a super spaceship under me. **(John Young)** What a feeling! What a view! **(Robert Crippen)** **Columbia's crew members, speaking from orbit on the first Space Shuttle mission.**

CHAPTER THREE

THE SHUTTLE FLEET

Columbia returned to orbit four more times before the next orbiter, Challenger, made its debut. Then, in turn, came Discovery and Atlantis. By the end of 1985, the Space Shuttle Fleet was complete, with the four orbiters taking turns flying into space.

After its triumphant maiden flight in April 1981, *Columbia* was examined in great detail back at the Kennedy Space Center. As well as the tiles missing from the tail pod, other tiles were damaged, and about one thousand eventually were replaced. This and other essential work on *Columbia* was completed by fall. Seven months after its first flight, *Columbia* was rolled out to the launchpad, ready for its second journey into space.

A launch attempt on November 4 ended just thirty-two seconds before liftoff because of problems with pressure in the fuel cells and in the APUs, or auxiliary power units. (The APUs provide power for the orbiter's hydraulic systems, which control such things as movement of the engine nozzles and operation of the landing gear.)

HISTORIC SECOND FLIGHT

The next launch attempt on November 12 was successful. *Columbia* punched its way into the skies for the second time. It was a unique occasion because no other spacecraft had ever flown into space twice.

▲ Columbia *begins its second flight into orbit (STS-2) on November 12, 1981. No craft had ever returned to space before.*

Astronauts Joe Engle and Richard Truly had a packed schedule for this *STS-2* mission. They tested the RMS, or robot arm, which would soon become an invaluable piece of equipment for payload operations. They also carried out experiments with the *Columbia*'s imaging radar, which scanned our planet's surface with radar beams (like those used on Earth to detect aircraft in the sky). The radar revealed interesting geological and archaeological features hidden beneath the surface. In Africa's Sahara Desert, *Columbia*'s ground-penetrating radar "saw" through the sand layers to reveal ancient river channels and the possible remains of Stone Age settlements.

Continuing problems with the fuel cells, which provided the orbiter's electrical power, led to *Columbia* returning after a little more than two days in space, rather than the five days planned.

▲ On Columbia's second flight, ground-imaging radar captured this image of the Los Angeles basin.

THE CANADARM

Another name for the RMS—the shuttle's remote manipulator system, or robot arm—is the Canadarm, because it was built in Canada (by Spar Aerospace). It measures about 50 feet (15 m) long and 15 inches (38 centimeters) in diameter. It has joints similar to those in a human arm: Its "shoulder" attaches to the payload bay; it has an "elbow" in the middle; a "wrist" farther down; and a "hand," called the end effector, at the tip. The end effector is fitted with wires that can grip fixtures on satellites and other payloads. Astronauts manipulate the arm by looking through windows on the orbiter's desk or by viewing the outside of the spacecraft on television monitors.

GOING COMMERCIAL

Columbia returned to space three more times the following year. On the third mission (STS-3, March 1982), it spent more than eight days in orbit. On this occasion, *Columbia* landed at White Sands Test Facility in New Mexico because the runway at the scheduled landing site—Edwards Air Force Base—was under inches of water. (White Sands is one of the Shuttle Fleet's alternate landing sites, and it has only been used once.) The fourth flight (*STS-4,* in June 1982) was the final test mission before the Shuttle began carrying commercial cargo. That flight, with more than thirty experimental payloads on board, went as planned.

On *STS-5* (November 1982), the Shuttle carried two communications satellites into space (*SBS-3* and *Anik-C3*) for commercial customers. The first was launched for a U.S. communications consortium called Satellite Business Systems. The second was launched for Telesat, a company that operates a domestic communications satellite system in Canada. NASA charged about $10 million for each launch. Astronauts William Lenoir and Joseph Allen oversaw the deployment of the satellites.

▲ The STS-5 crew members celebrate the successful launch of two communications satellites in November 1982. Clockwise from top left are Bill Lenoir, Bob Overmyer, Joe Allen, and Vance Brand.

Shuttle astronauts are called mission specialists. A new breed of astronaut, they are not necessarily pilots, but instead scientists, engineers, and medical specialists who perform mission objectives, such as satellite launches or EVA (extravehicular activities, or space walks). Malfunctions in the life-support backpacks on the space suits caused the cancellation of the EVAs scheduled for *STS-5*.

A WORTHY CHALLENGER

After its five pioneering flights, *Columbia* was scheduled for maintenance, and on April 4, 1983, a new Space Shuttle, *Challenger*, blasted off on mission *STS-6*. *Challenger* was named after a U.S. naval research vessel that sailed the Atlantic and Pacific Oceans in the 1870s.

The major payload operation on *Challenger's* maiden flight was the launch into geostationary orbit of the first tracking and data relay satellite (TDRS).

Circling in geostationary orbit, a number of TDRSs were planned to act as relay stations to handle communications between Shuttles, satellites, and ground stations. (In a geostationary orbit, a satellite travels at the same speed as Earth spins and so appears fixed in the same position in the sky.)

Mission specialists Story Musgrave and Donald Peterson needed to test out the space suits and tools for use on EVAs. They entered the air lock on *Challenger's* mid-deck, then floated out into its payload bay. Secured by tethers, or safety lines, they spent several hours in the Shuttle's bay practicing various repair missions.

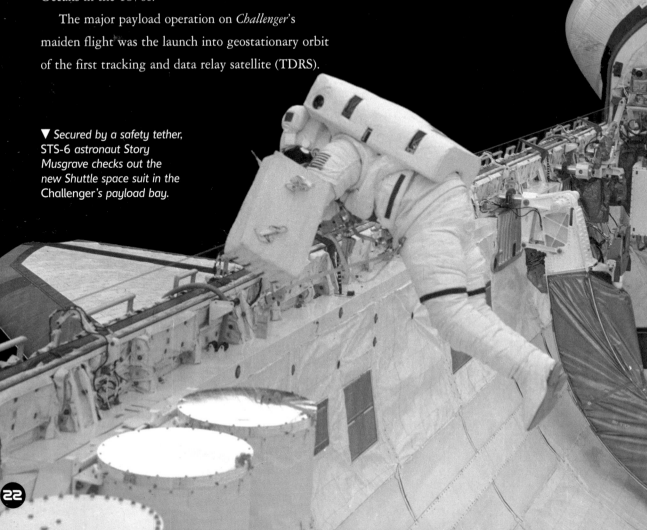

▼ Secured by a safety tether, STS-6 astronaut Story Musgrave checks out the new Shuttle space suit in the Challenger's payload bay.

Challenger's second mission (*STS-7*, June 1983) boasted a record crew of five and included the first U.S. female astronaut, Sally Ride.

FIRST LADIES

Until the flight of *Challenger* on mission *STS-7* (June 1983), all U.S. astronauts had been male. On this flight, Sally K. Ride (born in 1951) flew as a mission specialist. She returned to space on Mission *STS-41G* (October 1984). Judith A. Resnik (born in 1949) became the second U.S. female astronaut on the previous Shuttle flight (Mission *STS-41D*, August 1984). Tragically, Resnik, along with the entire crew, died on her second mission aboard *Challenger* in January 1986.

▼ *The first American woman in space, Sally Ride, peers through the windows of the payload station at the rear of* Challenger's *flight deck on STS-7.*

DISCOVERY AND ATLANTIS

The third Shuttle orbiter, *Discovery*, made its maiden voyage on August 30, 1984, on Mission *41D*. It was named after a ship in which Henry Hudson sailed in 1610, searching for a northwest passage between the Atlantic and Pacific Oceans. (Hudson Bay in Canada is named after him, as is the Hudson River in New York.)

▼ *On the twelfth Shuttle mission (STS-41D), communications satellite SBS-4 springs out of its pod in* Discovery's *payload bay. Its engine will later fire to thrust it into geostationary orbit, 22,300 miles (36,000 km) high. It is the first of three satellites launched on that mission.*

On *Discovery*'s debut mission, the crew launched a record three satellites, and the second U.S. woman in space, Judy Resnik, deployed a 100-foot (30-m) -long dummy solar array. It was the prototype for a large structure that would carry solar cells, devices that produce electricity from sunlight. Such an array could provide extra power for future long-duration Shuttle flights.

With the launch of *Atlantis* on a classified Department of Defense mission (*STS-51J*, October 1985), the Space Shuttle Fleet was complete. *Atlantis* is named after an ocean research sailing vessel operated by the Woods Hole Oceanographic Institute in Woods Hole, Massachusetts.

ORBITAL OPERATIONS

Life aboard the Space Shuttle proved a complete contrast from life in the cramped capsules of the early spacecraft. There was much more living space, with a galley (kitchen) to prepare food, a bathroom, and bunks to sleep on. Astronauts had never had it so good.

The astronauts who flew in Mercury, Gemini, and Apollo spacecraft had little room to move. They wore space suits, ate unappetizing gooey food from toothpaste-type tubes, could not wash properly, and had to use plastic bags when they went to the bathroom.

But when Shuttle astronauts went into orbit, they found living in space quite different. The crew accommodations on the upper and middle decks of the orbiter were relatively spacious. They breathed a normal nitrogen/oxygen atmosphere at a pleasant temperature in which they could wear ordinary clothes in comfort.

▲ Mark Brown juggles with food containers prior to preparing a meal for Columbia's crew in August 1989.

ON THE MENU

The menu for Shuttle meals was surprisingly varied. Most food was dehydrated, frozen, or canned, but was tasty when properly prepared. Dehydrated foods included macaroni and cheese, shrimp cocktail, and scrambled eggs. There was also fresh food, such as bananas, carrots, and celery, as well as juices, nuts, granola bars, and cookies. Meals could be taken on a tray and eaten with ordinary cutlery. Drinks could not be drunk in the ordinary way, however, because of the lack of gravity in orbit. Liquids had to be sucked up through straws.

WATER ON THE SHUTTLE

There is plenty of water available on a Shuttle. A sink provides running water by using a stream of air that causes it to flow. Excess water is sucked into a drain; otherwise, it would float around in the spacecraft's zero gravity.

JUST THE MEDICINE

Space medicine is a special branch of medicine that investigates the health effects of space travel. Muscle atrophy—a wasting away of muscle strength and tissue—is one of the known adverse health effects of weightlessness on the human body. Other effects include loss of bone matter and space sickness, or nausea. These effects are not a problem for most Shuttle travelers who spend only a few days in space, but they can develop into serious problems for astronauts who spend months in space—such as those living on space stations.

▲ Guion Bluford exercises on a treadmill on Challenger's mid-deck in August 1983 to help prevent muscle atrophy.

The Shuttle bathroom resembles the bathrooms astronauts use on Earth, but with added features, such as a seat belt and foot restraints. The toilet flushes using a stream of air, not water. Crew members take sponge baths using rinseless body-bath liquid and shampoo.

The astronauts sleep zipped up in sleeping bags attached to a padded bunk. They must be attached to something or, again, they would gradually float around. Two adjustable elastic straps stretching across each bag restrain the sleeping astronaut.

▼ Zipped into his sleeping bag, Norman Thagard snoozes on board Challenger in August 1983. In the weightless conditions, his arms float free.

LABORATORY IN SPACE

On the early Shuttle flights, the astronauts not only launched satellites but also carried out all kinds of experiments. These included processing biological and pharmaceutical samples and growing crystals. These experiments indicated that processing materials in zero gravity resulted in purer products and more perfect crystals. This could lead to better vaccines for medicinal use and better semiconductor materials for electronics equipment.

GETAWAY SPECIALS

Other experiments were flown as part of the so-called Getaway Specials (GAS) program. In this program, NASA provided standard-size containers in which customers housed their own experiments. The idea was to provide access to space for universities, research organizations, and schools at a reasonable cost—just a few thousand dollars.

The GAS containers were located on either side of the payload bay. They had to carry their own power and instruments and be designed to function independently. The first GAS flew on the fourth Shuttle flight. Provided by Utah State University, it included investigations into the effects of weightlessness on the growth rates of fruit flies, duckweed, and algae.

SPACELAB

The Shuttle orbiters were not specifically designed for experimental science, but some missions carried a fully equipped science laboratory, known as *Spacelab*, in their payload bay. Built by the European Space Agency, *Spacelab* made its space debut in December 1983 on Shuttle Mission *STS-9*, on the refurbished *Columbia*. That mission also included German physicist Ulf Merbold, the first European astronaut to fly on a U.S. spacecraft. Dr. Merbold,

▼ *Astronaut-scientists on the first* Spacelab *mission in December 1983. In the left foreground is German physicist Ulf Merbold, the first European to fly on a U.S. spacecraft. To his right are Byron Lichtenberg and Robert Parker.*

however, was not the first European astronaut. That honor belonged to Frenchman Jean-Loup Chrétien, who flew as a "guest cosmonaut" on the Soviet space station *Salyut 7* in June 1982. John Young, a veteran astronaut from the Gemini and Apollo eras and *STS-1* also flew aboard the *STS-9*. He was making his sixth spaceflight, a new record for indiviual space travel.

ESA

ESA, the European Space Agency based in Paris, France, is the organization that coordinates space activities in Europe. It was formed in 1975 from two former space organizations, ESRO (European Space Research Organization) and ELDO (European Organization for the Development and Construction of Space Vehicle Launchers). The fifteen member countries are Austria, Denmark, Belgium, Finland, France, Germany, Ireland, Italy, the Netherlands, Norway, Portugal, Spain, Sweden, Switzerland, and the United Kingdom.

This first *Spacelab* mission was highly successful. Over ten days, the astronauts conducted more than seventy experiments in biology and medicine, materials science, astronomy, and space physics. The medical experiments centered on research into the effects of weightlessness on the human body. Space-medicine experiments were also featured on other *Spacelab* flights, which continued into the 1990s.

SHUTTLE SPECTACULARS

Two months after *Columbia* returned from the *Spacelab 1* flight, *Challenger* took off on the first mission of 1984—a year that included some of the most spectacular space walking ever.

On this mission (*STS-41B*), the astronauts had a busy schedule. First, they launched two

▼ In the zero gravity of space, the six-member Spacelab 1 crew poses in a star formation in December 1983.

communications satellites (*Westar VI* and *Palapa B2*), which were then supposed to blast off into geostationary orbit 22,300 miles (32,900 km) high. Unfortunately, the satellites' booster rockets failed to ignite, stranding them in useless low orbits. Although NASA was not at fault, it was blamed for the mishaps anyway.

▲ An image of NASA astronauts' home base—Houston, Texas—taken by the crew on the Spacelab D-1 mission (STS-61A) in October 1985.

▲ Bruce McCandless flies free as he tests the manned maneuvering unit (MMU) during the STS-41B mission in February 1984. By firing the MMU's thrusters, McCandless finds he can maneuver in space with ease.

FLYING FREE

The next major objective of the *STS-41B* mission was the exciting test flight of a jet-propelled backpack. This device enabled astronauts to move around freely in space during EVAs. The backpack was called the MMU, or manned maneuvering unit.

Mission specialist Bruce McCandless wore the MMU first, then released his tether and fired the MMU's jet thrusters. He floated out of *Challenger*'s payload bay, hit the thrusters again, and ended up about 300 feet (91 m) away before returning. It was then Robert Stewart's turn to put the MMU through its paces.

The final triumph of *STS 41-B* came when *Challenger* made the first-ever Space Shuttle landing on the runway at the Kennedy Space Center.

> That may have been one small step for Neil, but it's a heck of a big leap for me.
> **Bruce McCandless, when he cast off his tether and began free flight in the MMU.**

THE MMU

MMU stands for manned maneuvering unit, a jet backpack that astronauts used on some of the most exciting EVAs of the Space Age. A prototype flew on space station *Skylab* in 1973, but the MMU made its first real flight on Shuttle Mission *STS-41B*. The MMU has been called a "flying armchair" because the astronaut rests his or her own arms on it. The back of the unit contains tanks of compressed nitrogen that feed sets of MMU thrusters. Using hand controls on the arms, the astronaut fires different sets of thrusters to move in different directions.

FIXING *SOLAR MAX*

Challenger Mission STS-41C was back in orbit two months later attempting something that had never been done before—the recovery and repair of a satellite. This satellite, *Solar Max* (Solar Maximum mission), had been launched four years earlier to study the Sun at a time of maximum activity, when solar flares and sunspots were at their peak. But it had been out of action for three years.

On the mission, *Challenger* flew to within 200 feet (60 m) of *Solar Max*, which was slowly spinning. George Nelson jetted over to it using the MMU. He planned to dock with *Solar Max* and then fire the MMU's jets to stop the satellite from spinning so that *Challenger*'s robot arm could capture it.

Unfortunately, Nelson was unable to dock. But the robot arm eventually managed to capture *Solar Max* and place it in the payload bay. The next day, Nelson and fellow space walker James van Hoften repaired the satellite. Another day later, *Solar Max* was back in orbit, working perfectly.

▲ STS-41C *astronaut George Nelson (seen here in white circle), rides on* Challenger*'s robot arm in April 1984 to inspect* Solar Max. *Earlier, he performed some spectacular space walking to recover the satellite.*

SALVAGING SATELLITES

Even more spectacular space walking came with the last flight of 1984 (Mission *STS-51A*), by *Discovery* in November. Pleased with the success in recovering and repairing *Solar Max*, NASA embarked on a plan to capture the two satellites lost in February—*Westar VI* and *Palapa B2*—and bring them back to Earth.

The plan called for an MMU-equipped astronaut to fly to each satellite and dock with it using a device (known as the stinger) that fitted into the satellite's rocket nozzle. The stinger had a grapple pin—a rod that the robot arm could grip to capture the satellite that needed repair.

Discovery rendezvoused first with *Palapa B2*. Then Joseph Allen flew over to it in the MMU and fixed the stinger to it. The robot arm grabbed it and positioned *Palapa B2* over *Discovery*'s payload bay. Then Allen and fellow space walker Dale Gardner wrestled the satellite into its berth in the bay. Two days later, Gardner flew the stinger to *Westar VI*, and again he and Allen berthed it in the payload bay by hand. The mission salvaged both satellites, with a total worth of about $150 million.

FIXING IT, AGAIN

The "fix-it" skills of Shuttle astronauts were also used during Mission *STS-51I* in August 1985. This time, the astronauts attempted an in-orbit repair of

▼ *On Mission STS-51A, astronauts Dale Gardner and Joseph Allen participate in some of the most spectacular space walking ever as they attempt to recover two satellites. Far left: Gardner flies the stinger to the* Westar. *Middle: Gardner (right) and Allen grab hold of the satellite. Right: Gardner mugs with a "For Sale" sign advertising the two captured satellites.*

Leasat 3, a satellite launched from *Discovery* four months earlier. The satellite had been marooned in low orbit after a major electrical circuit failure.

James van Hoften was the key figure in *Leasat 3*'s dramatic recovery. While riding on *Discovery*'s robot arm, van Hoften—nicknamed "Ox" because of his strength—literally grabbed the satellite and held it while the robot arm carried him back to *Discovery*'s payload bay. Fellow space walker William Fisher fitted a new electronics box to the satellite, which then sprang to life on command. The next day, van Hoften gave *Leasat 3* a twist to start its rotation and pushed it away, back into orbit: A Space Shuttle mission had just saved another $85 million satellite.

> This repair demonstrated the value of sending people into space, and I hope that reminds everybody of the Shuttle's capabilities.
> **NASA spokesman Jesse Moore, after the in-orbit repair of *Leasat 3* from STS-51I.**

CHAPTER FIVE

COUNTDOWN TO DISTASTER

After the spectacularly successful flights of the Space Shuttles in 1984 and 1985, the loss of *Challenger* in January 1986 shocked the United States and the world.

The year 1985 saw a remarkable nine Shuttle flights. Spaceflight seemed almost routine. Americans became complacent about their space triumphs. Spoiled by the seemingly effortless Space Shuttle missions, the American public ignored the basic fact that every spaceflight is very dangerous— literally an accident waiting to happen.

In January 1986, millions of schoolchildren eagerly awaited Space Shuttle Mission *STS-51L, Challenger*'s tenth flight. NASA and the media dubbed this the "teacher's flight" because for the first time, *Challenger* would carry a teacher, Christa McAuliffe. She was scheduled to give the first live lessons from space.

The *STS-51L* flight was postponed first because of a delayed previous Shuttle mission (*STS-61C*) and then because of technical problems and bad weather. Finally, NASA gave the go-ahead for the launch on January 28—despite temperatures plummeting below freezing the night before.

At 11:38 A.M. (local time), *Challenger* lifted off the launchpad into the sky. It seemed like a perfect launch: It was not. Seventy-three seconds into the flight, *Challenger* exploded in a gigantic fireball. Its crew of seven became the first in-flight casualties of the U.S. space program.

THE CHALLENGER 7

On its tenth mission, *Challenger* carried a crew of seven, including teacher Christa McAuliffe. The Shuttle astronauts included rookie Greg Jarvis, Ronald McNair (a veteran of Mission *STS-41B*), Ellison Onizuka (*STS-51C*), Judy Resnik (*STS-41D*), Francis R. (Dick) Scobee (*STS-41C*), and rookie Michael Smith. On January 28, 1986, these astronauts ". . . slipped the surly bonds of Earth to touch the face of God," quoted President Reagan.

▼ *The Challenger crew, front row from left: Mike Smith, Dick Scobee, and Ron McNair. Back row from left: El Onizuka, Christa McAuliffe, Greg Jarvis, and Judy Resnik.*

WHAT WENT WRONG?

Careful study of photographs taken of the launch and instrument data transmitted by the doomed Shuttle helped NASA determine how the disaster happened. As *Challenger* lifted off, hot gases from inside the right-hand SRB (Solid Rocket Booster) forced their way through the O-ring seals in the booster's bottom joint.

About one minute into the flight, a scorching blowtorch of flame emerged from the joint and began burning through the strut that fixed the right-hand SRB to the large external fuel tank. Within a few seconds, the strut failed. The SRB swung around and smashed into the external tank. Spilled fuel ignited, creating the giant fireball explosion witnessed by thousands at the launch site and millions who watched on television.

> We always knew there would be a day like this. We're dealing with speeds and powers and complexities we've never dealt with before.
> **Former U.S. astronaut John Glenn, speaking shortly after *Challenger* exploded.**

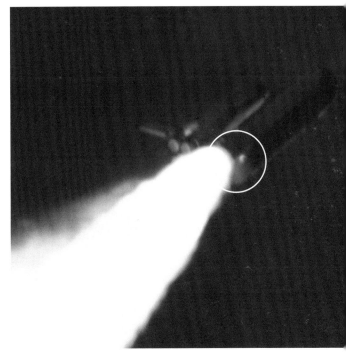

▲ *Just fifty-eight seconds after* Challenger *lifted off the launchpad on January 28, 1986, a plume of flame emerges from the lower part of its right-hand booster.*

THE ROGERS COMMISSION

As the nation mourned *Challenger*'s crew, President Reagan set up a commission to investigate the cause of the disaster. Headed by former Secretary of State William Rogers, the thirteen-member commission included first man on the Moon, Neil Armstrong, and the first American woman in space, Sally Ride.

The Rogers Commission identified failure of the O-ring joint seals as the main cause of the disaster; the freezing temperatures caused the seals to lose their ability to expand into the joint. The Commission discovered records of problems with the seals on previous flights, particularly when the Shuttle missions launched following freezing overnight temperatures.

▶ *Seventy-three seconds after liftoff,* Challenger *erupts in a fireball, from which only the still-firing rocket boosters emerge. The orbiter and crew are lost.*

OPPOSING THE LAUNCH

On the night before *Challenger*'s fateful launch, temperatures on the launchpad dropped way below freezing. Engineers from the booster's manufacturer, Thiokol, warned against the launch because they feared the O-rings would not seal properly. Rockwell, the orbiter manufacturer, also disagreed with the decision to launch because it feared that ice on the launch gantry would break off and damage *Challenger*'s heat-shield tiles. But these voices opposing the launch never got through to the top decision-making team, who gave the okay to launch.

In its report, the Rogers Commission not only recommended design changes to prevent a similar disaster, but also criticized NASA's management and lines of communication that allowed the launch to proceed despite reservations among members of the technical launch team.

▲ *President Ronald Reagan, speaking at a memorial service for the "Challenger Seven" at the Johnson Space Center, Houston, Texas.*

" . . .this America . . . was built by men and women like our seven star voyagers, who answered a call beyond duty. . . . Dick, Mike, Judy, El, Ron, Greg, and Christa—your families and your country mourn your passing. We bid you goodbye, but we will never forget you. "

President Ronald Reagan, 1986.

O-RINGS IN THE COLD

An experiment by Rogers Commission member Richard Feynman (1918–1988) provided a memorable and critical moment in the inquiry into the *Challenger* disaster. A leading physicist and Nobel prizewinner, Feynman demonstrated how the O-rings in the Shuttle's solid rocket boosters would have lost their flexibility at low temperatures. He compressed a piece of the rubberlike O-ring material in a clamp and immersed it in ice water. He pulled it out and undid the clamp. The O-ring material remained compressed for several seconds, showing it had lost its flexibility—and therefore its ability to seal—in the cold. In the commission's final report, Feynman outspokenly accused NASA of "playing Russian roulette" with astronauts' lives.

▲ *Ice on the launchpad gantry in the early morning of January 28, as* Challenger *awaits liftoff.*

A NEW BEGINNING

NASA grounded the Shuttle Fleet for more than two-and-a-half years while it overhauled its launch procedures and management structures and made extensive Shuttle system modifications. Eventually, a return-to-flight date for Space Shuttle *Discovery* was set for September 29, 1988.

The Shuttle spacecraft sitting on the launchpad that day included more than 400 changes from the Shuttle that had blown up, including 150 to the SRBs alone. The countdown ticked away, and just after 11:30 A.M. (local time), *Discovery* blasted off on Shuttle Mission *STS-26*. Kennedy Launch Control announced: "America returns to space as *Discovery* clears the tower."

Discovery's mission went exactly according to plan. The astronauts launched another tracking and data relay satellite to replace the one lost on *Challenger* and carried out a variety of experiments. By doing so, the mission demonstrated that the Shuttle was still a reliable Space Transportation System. When *Discovery* touched down at Edwards Air Force Base at the end

▲ Discovery *streaks from the launchpad in September 1988 on Mission STS-26. The Space Shuttle is returning to flight after being grounded for thirty-two months following the* Challenger *disaster.*

of its four-day flight, Mission Control at Houston observed: "A great ending to a new beginning."

A SOVIET SHUTTLE

In an attempt to steal the limelight, the Soviet Union chose *Discovery*'s launch day to announce to the world that it had its own shuttle. The first launch would take place in a month's time. The Soviets named their shuttle *Buran* ("Snowstorm"). *Buran* looked almost identical to the U.S. Space Shuttle. It was tile-covered with delta wings. But it did not have any main engines. Instead, the *Buran* was designed to launch into space on top of a powerful rocket called Energia. *Buran* itself had only small rocket engines to provide a final boost into orbit and to act as retrorockets. It was also the only reusable part of the launch vehicle. Although *Buran* was designed for manned flight, its first flight was unmanned.

Delayed since October 1988, it eventually blasted off on November 15 from the Baikonur Cosmodrome. After a two-orbit flight, *Buran* made a perfect landing close to its launch site. Said Radio Moscow: "The space plane has ushered in a new era in the history of Soviet space exploration."

Further flights, with a cosmonaut crew, were planned, and a second *Buran* was built. But no Soviet shuttle ever flew again. Strapped for cash, the Soviet Union decided to concentrate on its prime space

objective—permanently manned space stations. They had launched their latest space station, *Mir*, early in 1986, and some cosmonauts had already worked in it for almost a year.

BACKLOG

After the U.S. Shuttle Fleet returned to flight, Shuttle operations got slowly back on track. A backlog of spacecraft waited for launch. One was *Magellan*, a probe designed to orbit Venus and map its surface using radar. Originally scheduled for launch in 1988, Space Shuttle *Atlantis* carried it into space in May 1989. The *Hubble Space Telescope* (*HST*) was another spacecraft overdue for launch. Originally set for launch in 1986. Space Shuttle *Discovery* (Mission *STS-31*) finally placed the *HST* in orbit in April 1990.

A NEW *ENDEAVOUR*

The Shuttle Fleet got back to full strength with the flight of Space Shuttle *Endeavour*, the replacement for *Challenger*, named after British navigator and explorer Captain James Cook's first ship. Cook set sail aboard the *Endeavour* in 1768, voyaging across the Atlantic and Pacific Oceans to New Zealand and Australia.

Endeavour made a spectacular debut on May 7, 1992, on Mission *STS-49*, in which three astronauts space walked to capture an *Intelsat 6* communications satellite that had been marooned in low orbit for more than two years. The space walkers set a new EVA record of nearly eight-and-a-half hours.

Spectacular space walks were also the highlights of *STS-61* in December 1993. This was a make-or-break recovery and repair mission for the *Hubble Space Telescope*, which had proved to have faulty "vision" because of a manufacturing error. In EVAs totaling more than thirty-five hours, the crew installed a new mirror assembly, called COSTAR, to correct the

▲ Soviet Space Shuttle *Buran* sits on the launchpad, mounted on its powerful carrier rocket, Energia. Its similarity to the U.S. Space Shuttle is striking.

telescope's faulty vision. They also replaced the solar panels and fixed other systems. After it was redeployed into space, the *HST* worked perfectly and began returning the most incredible images of stars, nebulae (huge clouds of gas and dust), and galaxies astronomers had ever seen.

▲ *Three space walkers capture a huge communications satellite by hand during* Endeavour's *first flight into space in May 1992.*

▼ *At the end of its flawless maiden flight,* Endeavour *touches down on the runway at the Kennedy Space Center. It was the first Shuttle to use a parachute for braking after landing.*

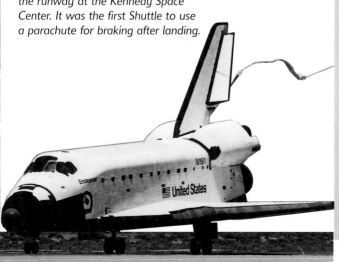

NEW WINDOW ON THE UNIVERSE

The *Hubble Space Telescope* (*HST*) is one of NASA's most successful spacecraft. Launched from Space Shuttle *Discovery* in 1990, the *HST* has returned some of the most spectacular images ever of our Universe. More than 43 feet (13 m) long and 14 feet (4.3 m) in diameter, it has a mass of more than 12 tons (10.8 tonnes). *Hubble* gathers light using a curved mirror 95 inches (2.4 m) across. Early images from the *HST* were blurred because the mirror had been ground with the wrong curvature. The *STS-61* repair mission in 1993 corrected this, and further servicing missions in 1997, 1999, and 2002 equipped the telescope with better instruments, which improved the quality of its images even more.

CHAPTER SIX

IN NEW DIRECTIONS

By 1995, NASA was heavily committed to another major space project—the construction of an International Space Station. In that year, astronauts began flying Shuttle missions to Russia's space station, *Mir*, to gain experience with space station life and operations.

Three of the seven Space Shuttle missions in 1995 were committed to joint flights with Russia. (Russia was by then a separate republic, not part of the Soviet Union.) These missions marked the beginning of a period of even closer cooperation between the U.S. and Russia in the construction of the upcoming *International Space Station* (*ISS*).

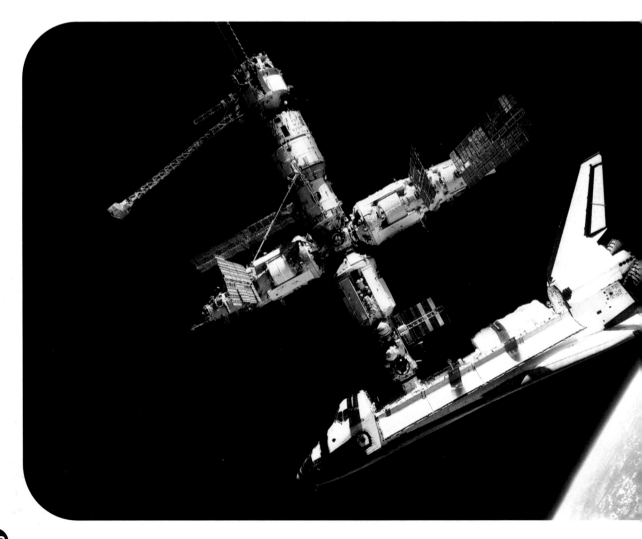

MIR

Mir was the last and most successful of a series of space stations sent into orbit by the Soviet Union. *Mir* was built in stages from modules (units) launched separately into orbit. The first module was launched in 1986; other modules were added between 1987 and 1996. The last manned mission to *Mir* took place in 2000. The *Mir* Space Station dropped out of orbit in March 2001.

In February 1995, *Discovery* Mission *STS-63* rendezvoused with Russia's space station *Mir*, which had been permanently occupied for nearly nine years. In June, *Atlantis* (*STS-71*) actually docked with *Mir*. The flight marked the one-hundredth U.S. manned space mission. *Atlantis* carried two new cosmonauts to *Mir* and carried the former three-man crew back to Earth. The returning crew members included U.S. astronaut Norman Thagard, who had spent three months on *Mir*.

There were nine *Mir*-Shuttle docking missions in all, the last in June 1998. Over the missions, seven U.S. astronauts gained valuable long-term experience in space on *Mir*, staying in orbit for an accumulated total of more than 900 days.

THE *INTERNATIONAL SPACE STATION*

As the Shuttle flights to *Mir* ended, the United States and Russia concentrated on developing the first modules that would form the *International Space Station*. Russia launched the first one, named *Zarya*, in November 1998; *Endeavour* carried up *Unity,* the first U.S. module and *Zarya*'s mate, a few weeks later.

Over the next five years, a succession of Russian Proton rockets and U.S. Space Shuttles launched new

◀ *Space Shuttle* Atlantis *links up with Russia's space station* Mir *in 1995.*

modules for the *ISS* and "Expedition" crews to man it. Russia's *Soyuz TM-31* spacecraft carried up the *Expedition 1* crew in October 2000; *Discovery* brought the *Expedition 2* crew just over four months later, returning with the *Expedition 1* crew.

EXTENDED MISSIONS

Like the other Space Shuttles, *Columbia* was involved in missions to the *International Space Station* (*ISS*). It also flew other kinds of missions as well. *Columbia* was equipped for long-duration missions and had set a Shuttle record in 1996 (Mission *STS-78*) of more than sixteen days in orbit.

On January 16, 2003, *Columbia* set off on its twenty-eighth mission (*STS-107*), aiming for an equally long stay in space. This was a dedicated science mission. Many experiments were conducted in a unit called *Spacelab* carried in the payload bay. The science went well. On day sixteen, February 1, *Columbia* fired its retrorockets and plunged back through the atmosphere, headed for its home base, the Kennedy Space Center. Touchdown was scheduled for about 9:15 A.M. (local time).

▼ *A space-walking astronaut at work on the construction of the* International Space Station. *More than 160 space walks will be required to completely assemble the* ISS.

THE UNTHINKABLE HAPPENS—AGAIN

Just before 9:00 A.M., *Columbia* was passing over northern Texas when Mission Control at Houston registered abnormally high temperature readings coming from temperature sensors on the left-hand side of the craft. Then the sensors quit working.

Mission Control alerted *Columbia*'s commander Rick Husband to the problem. He said "Roger" before all communications ceased. At that moment, *Columbia*, traveling at more than eighteen times the speed of sound, began disintegrating, leaving a trail of debris in the sky that was clearly visible to people on the ground.

Columbia, the very first U.S. Space Shuttle to fly in 1981, was lost. So was its crew: Rick Husband, William McCool, Michael Anderson, Kalpana Chawla, David Brown, Laurel Clark, and Israeli payload specialist Ilan Ramon.

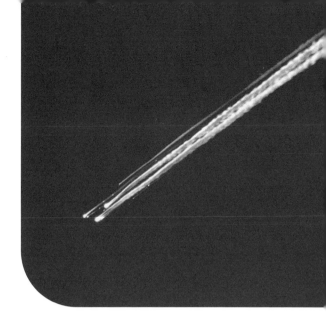

▲ The destruction of Columbia *in the skies above Texas on February 1, 2003. The orbiter has broken into pieces.*

Yet again, the illusion that space travel was becoming routine—and safe—was shattered. *Columbia* was another sad reminder that space travel is always dangerous and sometimes deadly.

THE FATAL LAUNCH

Much like the doomed *Challenger* seventeen years earlier, *Columbia*'s fate was sealed within seconds of liftoff. A chunk of insulation tore off the external fuel tank, striking and splitting open one of the reinforced carbon panels on the leading edge of the *Columbia*'s left wing. These panels were designed to protect *Columbia*'s aluminum airframe from the fiercest reentry heating.

When *Columbia* eventually reentered the atmosphere, searing hot air penetrated the split panel, melting the aluminum structure underneath. The wing crumpled, and aerodynamic forces then tore the entire spacecraft apart.

◄ The crew of Columbia's final mission (STS-107). *In the front row, from left to right, are David Brown, Rick Husband, and Michael Anderson. William McCool is in the middle. Laurel Clark, Ilan Ramon, and Kalpana Chawla are at the back.*

CAIB RECOMMENDATIONS

After the loss of *Columbia*, NASA grounded the Space Shuttle Fleet. The Columbia Accident Investigation Board (CAIB), under the chairmanship of retired Admiral Harold Gehman, investigated the tragedy and reported to President George W. Bush in August 2003. The CAIB report included twenty-nine recommendations, fifteen of which were mandatory before a Shuttle could fly again. These measures will help prevent the loss of insulation from the external tank and assure improved imaging of the Shuttle during launch and in orbit in order to assess any damage to the heat-shielding materials. Future Shuttle flights also need to carry equipment suitable for use while the Shuttle remains in orbit.

> Today, the Columbia Accident Investigation Board released its report on the tragic accident that claimed the lives of seven brave astronauts. These men and women assumed great risk in service to all humanity. On behalf of a grateful nation, I once again recognize their sacrifices and those of their loved ones. . . . Our journey into space will go on. The work of the crew of the *Columbia* and the heroic explorers who traveled before them will continue.
>
> **President George W. Bush, after receiving the CAIB's report.**

NASA CRITICIZED

Could *Columbia* have been saved? In hindsight, inspection of *Columbia* in orbit by a space-walking astronaut might have alerted NASA to the damaged tiles, but there was no indication at the time that such a heat-shield inspection was needed.

The CAIB also criticized NASA for its structure, management, decision-making processes, and unfounded "self-confident outlook of it having a unique knowledge about how to safely launch people into space." NASA Administrator Sean O'Keefe accepted the recommendations and agreed to take steps to overhaul the agency.

▼ *In the* Columbia *RLV (reusable launch vehicle) hangar, engineers begin the task of identifying the debris that fell to Earth after* Columbia *broke up.*

SHUTTLING INTO THE FUTURE

Another observation made by the Columbia Accident Investigation Board was that the existing Space Shuttles cannot be operated safely for many more years and that they should be replaced as soon as possible. What, then, is waiting to replace them? The short answer is: nothing—yet.

NASA is, however, pursuing research into the development of spacecraft that complement, rather than replace, the Space Shuttle Fleet. Called the OSP, or Orbital Space Plane, this new spacecraft could come into operation sometime after the year 2010.

CREW CARRIER

The OSP is a much simpler vehicle than the Shuttle and is designed to carry a crew, but not a payload. The Shuttle was designed to carry crews and payloads. Its large payload bay makes it the space vehicle of choice for lifting into orbit sections of the *ISS*. Once the *ISS* is complete, the Shuttle Fleet will

be an expensive way of ferrying crews to and from the *ISS*. The decision to build a dedicated crew carrier follows current thinking that space vehicles serve a specific purpose: for example, to launch a crew or to launch a satellite—but not both. The OSP will function both as a means of transporting crews to and from the *ISS* and also as a crew return vehicle (CRV) in an emergency. Much CRV development work has already been carried out by the X-38 program—which NASA halted when it decided to develop the more versatile OSP.

Other countries have considered similar launch systems. The European Space Agency came up with a manned space plane called *Hermes*, and Japan proposed an unmanned vehicle called *Hope*. Like the OSP, *Hermes* and *Hope* are intended for missions to and from the *ISS*, in which Europe and

▼ *A flight test through the atmosphere of a scale model of the X-38 in July 1999. It has just been dropped from a B-52 aircraft.*

Japan are major participants. But both projects are on hold while the ESA and Japan concentrate on fulfilling their commitments to the *ISS*.

▲ *The European space plane* Hermes *is shown docked with the* International Space Station *in this 1999 artist's rendition. The* Hermes *is basically a lifting-body design.*

FUTURE RLVs

Plans for a reusable launch vehicle (RLV) to replace the Space Shuttle have existed for a long time. NASA's Advanced Transportation Program is now responsible for defining and developing a new RLV. Its aim is the development of "spaceliners" that will launch and land at "aerospace ports" and be "as safe as today's commercial aircraft." Whether RLVs will ever be built is uncertain, for the future of space flight itself is uncertain.

SPACE BUDGET

Current spending on research into future launch vehicles like the OSP and RLVs averages about $1.7 billion a year. This represents about 11 percent of

NASA's current budget of about $15 billion. Spending on the *International Space Station* is about the same. By comparison, the Space Shuttle program consumes more than $5 billion annually, or more than 30 percent of the total budget.

Phasing out the Shuttle and switching to more economical methods of sending crews into space should therefore bring about considerable savings, but resources might well be switched to other projects. More funding may go to space science, for example, which is presently concerned with robot exploration of the Solar System using planetary probes (current budget: $4 billion).

Or, the resources might go toward developing interplanetary vehicles to support manned Moon missions and even manned missions to Mars. President Bush indicated his support for such future missions in a speech at NASA headquarters in January 2004. (A manned Mars mission would probably cost somewhere around $600 billion.)

▲ *The X-37 craft, seen in this artist's impression, has been designed as an advanced technology flight demonstrator for the Orbital Space Plane. Flight tests in the atmosphere could take place in 2004, with an orbital test flight following as early as 2006.*

1961

April 12: Soviet cosmonaut Yuri Gagarin in the spacecraft *Vostok 1* becomes the first person to orbit the Earth.

May 5: Alan Shepard becomes the first U.S. astronaut when he makes a suborbital flight in *Freedom 7*.

1962

February 20: John Glenn becomes the first American into orbit, circling the Earth three times in *Friendship 7*.

1965

March 18: Cosmonaut Alexei Leonov makes the world's first space walk from *Voskhod 2*.

June 3: Edward White makes the first U.S. space walk from *Gemini 4*.

1969

April: President Nixon asks NASA to plan the future in space; NASA decides to give priority to a reusable Space Transportation System, or Shuttle Fleet.

July 20: *Apollo 11* lands on the Moon. Neil Armstrong is the first man to walk on the Moon.

1972

January 5: President Nixon approves development of the reusable Space Shuttle Fleet.

December: The final Apollo mission, *Apollo 17*) returns from the Moon.

1977

Prototype Shuttle Orbiter *Enterprise* completed.

February: Unmanned, "captive" Shuttle flight tests on top of a Boeing 747 aircraft begin.

August: The first manned, "free" Shuttle flight tests begin.

1979

March: The first operational Space Shuttle, *Columbia*, arrives at the Kennedy Space Center.

1981

April 12: *Columbia* ushers in the Space-Shuttle era when it takes to the skies (Mission *STS-1*) for a 54-hour trip into space. It returns to space on November 12, 1981 (Mission *STS-2*).

1982

November 11: The first commercial Space Shuttle flight takes place on Mission *STS-5*.

1983

April 4: The second Space Shuttle, *Challenger*, launches (Mission *STS-6*).

June: Sally Ride becomes the first American woman to fly into space (Mission *STS-7*).

December: The European-built *Spacelab* makes its debut on Mission *STS-9*.

1984

February: Bruce McCandless becomes the first "human satellite," flying freely in the manned maneuvering unit (MMU) on Mission *STS-41B*.

April: On *STS-41C*, *Challenger*'s astronauts capture and repair the *Solar Max* satellite.

August: The third Space Shuttle, *Discovery*, makes its maiden flight on *STS-41D*.

October: On *STS-41G*, Kathryn Sullivan becomes the first U.S. woman to make a space walk.

1985
October 3: The fourth Space Shuttle, *Atlantis*, launches (Mission *STS-51J*).

1986
January 28: *Challenger* explodes 73 seconds after liftoff on Mission *STS-51L*, killing its crew of seven. All Shuttle flights are suspended.

1987
August: U.S. Congress approves the construction of a new Shuttle Orbiter to replace *Challenger*.

1988
September 29: Shuttle flights resume with the launch of *Discovery* (Mission *STS-26*).

November 15: Soviet Space Shuttle *Buran* blasts off from the Baikonur Space Center. Its unmanned, two-orbit flight is its first and last.

1992
May 7: Replacement Space Shuttle *Endeavour* blasts off on its maiden voyage (Mission *STS-49*).

1993
December: *Discovery's* (*STS-61*) astronauts carry out a daring repair mission to correct the "flawed vision" of the *Hubble Space Telescope*.

1994
February: *Discovery* launches on *STS-60*, carrying Sergei Krikalev, the first Russian cosmonaut to fly aboard a U.S. spacecraft.

1995
February: *Discovery* carries out a rendezvous in orbit with the Russian space station, *Mir*.

June: *Atlantis* makes the first of nine Space Shuttle dockings with *Mir*.

1996
March: Shannon Lucid flies in *Atlantis* (*STS-76*) to *Mir* for a long-term mission. She returns in *Atlantis* (*STS-79*) in September after 188 days—the longest mission in space (at that time) by a U.S. astronaut.

1998
November: Construction of the *International Space Station* (*ISS*) begins with the launch of the Russian module, *Zarya*. *Endeavour* ferries up the first U.S. module, *Unity*, in December (*STS-88*).

2000
October: A Soyuz spacecraft ferries up the *Expedition 1* crew to take up residence in the *ISS*.

2003
February 1: *Columbia* breaks up in the atmosphere when returning to Earth after a 16-day mission (*STS-107*). The crew of seven is lost, and the entire Space Shuttle Fleet is grounded.

astronautics
The science of space travel.

attitude
The way a spacecraft is orientated, (positioned) in space.

capsule
The crew compartment of early spacecraft.

communications blackout
The normal suspension of communications between a spacecraft's crew and Mission Control that happens during reentry.

countdown
The backward counting of time to launch time (T) of a space rocket. "T-5" (pronounced "T minus 5"), means five minutes before liftoff.

docking
The joining up of two spacecraft in space.

EVA (ExtraVehicular Activity)
Time spent outside a spacecraft while in space; also known as space walking.

expendable
Used once and discarded.

external tank
The part of the Space Shuttle that carries fuel for its engines.

fuel cells
Units used on the Space Shuttle that produce electricity by combining hydrogen and oxygen.

heat shield
A coating on the outside of a spacecraft that protects it from the heat generated during reentry into the atmosphere.

lifting body
A flying craft with a body shape that helps it develop lift—an upward force that helps support the craft in the air.

Mission Control
The center that controls the flight of a spacecraft and crew activities in space.

MMU (Manned Maneuvering Unit)
a powered backpack used by astronauts to move freely in outer space.

NASA
National Aeronautics and Space Administration.

orbit
The usually circular or elliptical path in space taken by an object around a celestial body.

orbiter
The part of the Space Shuttle that carries the crew and payload.

payload
The cargo a spacecraft carries.

propellant
A substance burned in a rocket to produce the hot gases that propel it.

prototype
A model or mock-up used to test a design concept.

reentry
The period during which a spacecraft returns to the Earth's atmosphere.

rendezvous
The meeting of two spacecraft in space.

retrorocket
A rocket fired to slow down a spacecraft. A spacecraft fires its retrorockets as a brake to reduce its speed or to reorient itself.

rocket
An engine that burns fuel in oxygen to produce hot gases. As the gases shoot out backward through a nozzle, the rocket is propelled forward, by reaction. Rockets work in space because they carry their own oxygen supply.

SRBs
Solid rocket boosters; the two reusable booster rockets that provide the main thrust at liftoff for the Space Shuttles.

thrusters
Small rockets on a spacecraft fired to help maneuver the craft in space.

weightlessness
The strange state astronauts experience in orbit, when their bodies—and everything else—appear to have no weight at all.

BOOKS TO READ

Bredeson, Carmen. **Living on a Space Shuttle.** Children's Press, 2003.

Furniss, Tim. **Atlas of Space Exploration.** Gareth Stevens Publishing, 2000.

Godwin, Robert. **Space Shuttle—NASA Mission Reports.** Apogee Books, 2001.

Harrington, Phillip, and Roger Ressmeyer. **Space Shuttle—A Photographic History.** Browntrout Publications, 2003.

Hawcock, David. **Amazing Pop-Up, Pull-Out Space Shuttle.** DK Publishing, 1998.

Heppenheimer, T.A. **Development of the Space Shuttle.** Smithsonian Books, 2002.

Peebles, Curtis, and Martin Thompson. **Flying Without Wings: NASA Lifting Bodies.** Smithsonian Books, 1999.

Schafer, Christopher. **The Space Shuttle Columbia Explosion.** Abdo Press, 2004.

SPACE CAMPS

Florida, Alabama, and other locations host a number of space camps in the summer months. Lessons include learning about the nature and problems of spaceflight as well as "hands-on" experience in spaceflight simulators.
www.spacecamp.com
www.vaspaceflightacademy.org

PLACES TO VISIT

Space Shuttles are launched from Cape Canaveral Air Force Station on Merritt Island, just inland from Cape Canaveral, Florida.

Guided bus tours of the launch facilities at the Kennedy Space Center and the Cape Canaveral Air Force Station occur daily.

For details of upcoming events, check out the following web sites:
www.nasa.gov/; www.ksc.nasa.gov/; and www.pao.ksc.nasa.gov/kscpao/schedule/schedule.htm.

The Johnson Space Center in Houston, Texas, has a visitors' center and rocket park. It is also home base for U.S. astronauts. For further details, see www.jsc.nasa.gov/ and http://spacecenter.org/.

Other air and space museums around the United States include:

International Women's Air and Space Museum, Cleveland, OH www.iwasm.org/

Intrepid Sea-Air-Space Museum, New York City www.intrepidmuseum.org/

Neil Armstrong Air and Space Museum, Wapakoneta, OH www.ohiohistory.org/places/armstron/

Oregon Air and Space Museum, Eugene, OR www.oasm.org/

Pima Air and Space Museum, Tucson, AZ www.pimaair.org/

San Diego Aerospace Museum, San Diego, CA www.aerospacemuseum.org/

The Smithsonian National Air and Space Museum (**NASM**), Washington, D.C. Exhibits include rockets and spacecraft such as Mercury, Gemini, and Apollo. www.nasm.edu/

U.S. Space and Rocket Center, Huntsville, AL www.ussrc.com

Virginia Air and Space Center, Hampton, VA www.vasc.org/

WEB SITES

The Columbia Disaster—Learn more details. www.nationmaster.com/encyclopedia/Space-Shuttle-Columbia-disaster

Hubble—View a gallery of celestial images and more. http://hubblesite.org/

International Space Station—Take a virtual visit. http://spaceflight.nasa.gov/station/flash/modules.html

NOVA—A look at remote-sensing technology. www.pbs.org/wgbh/nova/zeugma/tools.html

PBS Space Stations—View new frontiers in space. www.pbs.org/spacestation/

Spaceplanes—See cutting-edge space technology. www.fas.org/spp/military/program/launch/msp.htm

TIME magazine's report on *Challenger* www.time.com/time/reports/space/disaster1.html

ABOUT THE AUTHOR
Robin Kerrod writes on space and astronomy for a wide audience. In such best-selling titles as *Hubble, Apollo, Voyager,* and *Illustrated History of NASA*, he has chronicled the exciting human adventures into the space frontier.
Kerrod is a former winner of Britain's prestigious COPUS science book prize.